MW01181793

Believe in Yourself

Believe in Yourself

Pastor Deborah Wofford

Copyright © 2011 by Pastor Deborah Wofford.

Library of Congress Control Number: 2011908808
ISBN: Hardcover   978-1-4628-7985-4
               Softcover   978-1-4628-7984-7
               Ebook   978-1-4628-7986-1

All rights reserved. No part of this book may be reproduced or transmitted in any form or by any means, electronic or mechanical, including photocopying, recording, or by any information storage and retrieval system, without permission in writing from the copyright owner.

This book was printed in the United States of America.

To order additional copies of this book, contact:
Xlibris Corporation
1-888-795-4274
www.Xlibris.com
Orders@Xlibris.com
100227

BELIEVE IN YOURSELF

Genesis 1:1 in the beginning God created the heaven and earth.
It's time for you to realize what your dreams are worth.
Everyone can't see your dreams or what's in your heart.
God created you to be extra ordinary right from the start.
There isn't another person like you you're one of a kind.
It's time to live your dream I finally decided to live mine.
Have you really thought about what you wanna be?
Believe in yourself you can build and run your own company.
The people that called you a loser will be calling you boss.
Focus on the future; forget all the things you already lost.
You can create a new and improved way to take an x-ray.
Believe in yourself go after your dream starting today.
Dream big you can be a doctor and you can be a nurse.
All you gotta do is figure out what you gotta do first.
I'm here to plant a seed and help you give birth to your dream.
You're still a winner even if your own the losing team.
Take time to read before you know it you'll be a famous writer.
You can be a hero just picture yourself being a fire fighter.
Take time to think let your thoughts become a real live dream.
Do let negative people steal your joy or your Self Esteem.
Take a few minutes to think about what you really wanna do.
Start looking in the mirror everyday saying I believe in you.

The Old Testament	Abbreviations
Nahum	Nah
Habakkuk	Hab
Zephaniah	Zep
Haggai	Hag
Zechariah	Zech
Malachi	Mal
Matthew	Matt.
Mark	Mk
Luke	Lk
John	Jn
Acts	Acts
Romans	Rom.
1 Corinthians	1 Cor
2 Corinthians	2 Cor
Galatians	Gal
Ephesians	Eph
Philippians	Phil
Colossians	Col
1 Thessalonians	1 Thess
2 Thessalonians	2 Thess
1Timothy	1 Tim
2 Timothy	2 Tim
Titus	Ti
Philemon	Phim
Hebrews	Heb
James	James
1 Peter	1 Pet
2 Peter	2 Pet
1 John	1 Jn
2 John	2 Jn
3 John	3 Jn
Jude	Jude
Revelation	Rev

The Old Testament	Abbreviations
Genesis	Gen.
Exodus	Ex
Leviticus	Lev
Number	Num
Deuteronomy	Deut
Joshua	Josh
Judges	Jgs
Ruth	Ru
1 Samuel	1 Sam
2 Samuel	2 Sam
1 Kings	1 Kin
2 Kings	2 Kin
1 Chronicles	1 Chr
2 Chronicles	2 Chr
Ezra	Ezr
Nehemiah	Neh
Ester	Ester
Job	Job
Psalms	Ps
Proverbs	Prov
Ecclesiastes	Eccl
Songs of Solomon	Song
Isaiah	Is
Jeremiah	Jer
Lamentations	Lam
Ezekiel	Ezek
Daniel	Dan
Hosea	Hos
Joel	Joel
Amos	Amos
Obadiah	Obad
Jonah	Jon
Micah	Mic

Introduction

This book is dedicated to Dayjah and Jalen they faced a bully one day.
In remembrance of Amber Hilker the angel that had her life taken away.
Amber Hilker had to be going through pure agony and strife.
She touched so many lives, a lot of people are sad that she lost her life.
No one knew she was hurting or falling completely apart.
I never knew her but her story surely touched my heart.
I dedicate this to her mother and others that suffered that pain.
If her story touches one life then her death won't be in vain.
I dedicate this to every child facing a bully and hiding their tears.
I want you to know everyone in the world has some type of fears.
Stay strong I pray God's love replace all your fears and doubt.
I'm glad my children Dayjah and Jalen found the courage to speak out.
Once you've cried all night long you will encounter joy tomorrow.
I lived with a bully for ten years I suffered great pain and sorrow.
Heartaches made me feel like I would fade away and die.
I didn't feel like life was worth living if all I could do was cry.
After long sleepless night I finally decided to face all my grief.
I guess all the tears brought me some form of peace and relief.
Starting this day I wanna replace your pain with a living dream.
I wanna encourage you to hold your head high with Self Esteem.
Everybody take a breath believe in yourself hope is still in range.
If you're a bully please have a little consideration for a change.
It's time for you to realize success is still within your reach.
We all need to live by example and practice what we preach.
I can help change the world one small act at a time each day.
From this day forward believe in yourself success is on the way.
Believe in yourself my friend live each day as if it was your last day.

Exodus 20:3 Thou shalt have no other gods before me.
I love the Lord I tell him everyday Lord I really adore thee.
If you like children you might consider being a pediatrician.
You can keep children healthy and teach them about nutrition.
If you like to eat think about being a phenomenal cook.
Then you can put all your famous recipes in a book.
It doesn't matter if your dream is big or small or even gigantic.
Smile you're God's child you'll make a brilliant mechanic.
If you like helping others please consider being a teacher.
Don't run from God when and if he calls you to be a preacher.
Believe in yourself you got one life you gotta live your dream.
Don't let troubles hold you back move on after you scream.
If someone calls you dumb prove to yourself you're smart.
Believe in yourself don't forget to trust your own heart.
You'll fail if you don't believe, like a bird can't fly without wings.
Some people can be cruel they can say some ugly things.
I know personally words hurt they sink deeper day after day.
It's hard not to be bothered by the things other people say.
People will hurt you to get a laugh and call you ugly and fat.
I don't see the need for people to talk to other people like that.
Don't be afraid to tell someone when others are bullying you.
Don't let other people's opinion of you control what you do.
I know it can be hard to focus and keep a positive attitude.
Some times it's hard to understand why others are rude.
Keep believing in yourself don't let nothing ever interrupt.
You can accomplish anything if you just don't give up.

Leviticus 26:6 and I will give peace in the land.
The Lord will make you fearless to all man.
God can change things for you no matter what God is able.
Whatever you do don't let other people give you a label.
God created heaven and earth we should show him respect.
Your faith is based on the things you believe and expect.
It's time for you to live your life to the fullest without regret.
I'm sure you're not the only one that, wanna be a space cadet.
I know a few people that have a dream of being an astronaut.
Whatever you decide to be in life you gotta give it all you got.
I know one day you'll end up being a really good doctor.
I betcha one day you'll make a really good photographer.
Lawyers make good money I bet you'll make a good attorney.
Imma encourage you I bet you can learn a few things from me.
I want you to learn to love yourself and turn the other cheek.
If you ignore sarcastic people it doesn't mean you're weak.
Concentrate on your dreams like being a meteorologist.
Maybe you should think about being a cosmetologist.
You gotta ask yourself what does a bully really sees in you.
Maybe they are jealous of the wonderful things you can do.
The first thing you need to do is tell someone what's wrong.
Do whatever you gotta do to make the bully leave you alone.
A bully will keep bothering you until you make them go away.
Remember what goes around will come back around one day.
I really think all bullies need a taste of their own medicine.
Something will happen soon they won't bother you again.

Believe in Yourself

Numbers 6:25 The Lord makes his face shine upon thee.
In other words the Lord decided to be gracious unto me.
You gotta be courageous if you wanna be a police.
You gotta serve the Lord if you really want peace.
Believe in yourself you are my daughter you are my son.
Think about your future before you pick up that gun.
Before you take action think because your future is at stake.
On the other hand God watches every step you take.
I can't believe your dream is to grow up and go to jail.
Don't miss your once in a life time chance to go to the NF.L.
I think it's time for you to start living your life today.
If you work real hard you can make it to the N.B.A.
It's time for you to start loving yourself the way you are.
You can still wake up one day and be a super star.
Every thought you have can end up being your dream.
Believe me I use to take all my thoughts to the extreme.
I don't think you should let your role model be a drug dealer.
Believe me negative people can really be a real dream killer.
It's hard to think positive with native thoughts in your head.
In other words you can't kill what appears to already be dead.
Ask yourself what it takes to make your dream come alive.
I want you to look in the mirror and get ready to thrive.
I want you to find away to release anger and stress.
No matter what you do I want you to give it your best?
Believe in yourself you got your whole life ahead of you.
Today I want you to start thinking about something new.

Deuteronomy 31:6 be strong and of good courage fear not.
God loves you in case you didn't know or in case you forgot.
The Lord didn't create you to be bullied or mistreated.
A bully is no longer a bully once he's been defeated.
Don't be afraid get someone to make the bully back off you.
Bullies run when someone bigger comes along and say boo.
I lived in a house with a bully for years he was an abusive pig.
People abuse others to make their self look and feel big.
I don't want you to let a bully push you over the edge.
Believe in yourself I believe in you that's my solemn pledge.
I wanna encourage you I wanna erase your pain and tears.
I really hope and pray something I say eases all your fears.
I know the Lord can take all the weight off your shoulders.
I really believe one day you and I will make good soldiers.
Once the bully is off your back you'll be a great entrepreneur.
I wanna show you compassion for the pain you've endured.
If you set your mind to it you can be a great accountant.
The first thing you really need to do is stop saying I can't.
I want you to write your thoughts down then make a list.
Can you picture yourself running your own business?
Take time to ask yourself do you wanna be a business owner.
Don't let your so called friends cause you to be a loner.
Don't live someone else's dreams you gotta live your own.
Believe in yourself dream big live your life before it's gone.
I really love helping people process all their pain and grief.
The Lord gives me joy when I see others feel a sigh of relief.

Joshua 1:9-Be strong and of good courage be not afraid.
The Lord already forgave you for the mistakes you made.
I know what it feels like to feel alone for a long time I felt odd.
The best thing you can do is turn your bully over to God.
One day my abuser tried to kill me so he was almost a killer.
At that point I started day dreaming about being a car dealer.
I let my mind wonder I thought about being a police chief.
I had to do something to get my mind off my pain and grief.
My husband was a bully he put my heart through the wringer.
I really wish I could sing the blues but I'm not a good singer.
I found this place in my mind where my heart can dance.
I started dreaming and believing in myself so I took a chance.
I'm not afraid of water but still I don't know how to swim.
I thought about jumping in calling the Lord and trusting him.
I don't think I would do it especially without a life guard.
My faith is just that strong because I really trust God.
I retired a few years ago I use to be a fabulous drama queen.
Now I'm enjoying helping others give birth to their dream.
Hold your head up you gotta dream living inside of you.
You'll make a great actor or actress I thought you knew.
Believe in yourself you can make it happen I know you can.
I remember learning to crawl before I learned how to stand.
You were born because God gave you a reason to live.
Start with a little soul searching then try being a detective.
You'll find something wonderful if you let your mind travel.
Whatever you do don't ever let a bully see you unravel.

Judges 6:25 and it came to pass the same night.
When the Lord takes care of you problems he will get it right.
The Lord can feel your discomfort and the things that bother you.
When you least expect it the Lord will show up and come though.
It's hard to be happy when you're life seems to be unhappy and sad.
The Lord always shows up when everything really looks bad.
When someone constantly tortures you it takes your joy way.
It feels like a huge piece of you is torn in half day after day.
I know exactly how it feels to feel invisible in a crowed room.
With a smile painted on your face you still feel pretty gloom.
You gotta stop crying and start praying yourself to sleep at night.
Just because a person say their sorry don't make things right.
Sometimes you feel like a pond in a no ending game up chest.
No matter what takes place everyone always knows what's best.
It seems like you're screaming loud and no one can hear you.
Now you're filled with so much anger but no one has a clue.
You're feeling like no one will see you unless you go over board.
You need to pray even harder because evil has its own reward.
Don't fly off the handle that's what the devil wants you to do.
The Lord has his eye on your enemy the Lord is watching you.
The Lord will fight your battles he will handle your enemy.
One day they will look back at you and see nothing but envy.
That time has come and you can believe that the time is very near.
God will make you a giant and make your enemies live in fear.
The Lord will cause your hurt and pain to fade away.
Just remember wonderful things happen every time you pray.

Believe in Yourself

Ruth 2:13-she said let me find favor in thy sight, my Lord.
Ruth found favor because she obeyed God she found her reward.
Imagine yourself talking to God and he answered you like that.
Don't worry about other people pay attention where you're at.
Don't let anyone steal your life and take the love out of you.
Give your heart to the Lord and wait for your breakthrough.
How in the world can you fall when you're already down?
Humble yourself under God and he's turn things around.
Life can be hard but the Lord has the power to make it easy.
After going through so must pain the Lord really saved me.
Nightmares surrounded me and kept me scare out of my mind.
I was awake through most of my nightmares I felt totally blind.
When someone is bothering you it can drive you insane.
You won't understand unless you on the receiving end of the pain.
I learned how to escape my pain by going to a place in my mind.
I told myself once it was all over everything would be just fine.
The fact of the matter is abuse in any form is never okay.
I remember when I endured some type of abuse every single day.
My days grew longer and my nights grew really ugly and cold.
It seemed my abuse would never end and the torture grew old.
Now that my Self Esteem was gone I felt hope and despair.
I wouldn't have made it without God's love and prayer.
I'm happy now I have songs of praise singing in my heart.
I can't believe no one saw me falling completely apart.
The Lord gave me strength to stand up on my own two feet.
When I was invisible to the world God made me complete.

1 Samuel 2:34 and this shall be a sign unto thee.
Believe in yourself God will speak to you by using me.
I made mistakes when I was a child I made more as I got older.
No matter what God always took the weight off my shoulder.
I was totally amazed when God showed me my true identity.
I'm glad God let his loving and amazing spirit resides in me.
I wanna help you find your true identity by helping you cope.
I'll help you learn to believe in yourself by giving you hope.
You gotta stop being afraid and take the bullies power away.
There is power in the word of God start using it today.
When your bully calls you names tell them God still loves me.
The day you stop showing you care is the day you break free.
I know that pain hurts because I felt that type of pain before.
Hide your emotions and the bully won't bother you any more.
Bullies get off by seeing others expression of hurt and pain.
Believe me those emotions can literally drive you insane.
But you can't hold all those emotions and frustrations in.
You can break free by telling someone; don't let the bully win.
You are special and you got some beautiful dream to fulfill.
The main thing you need to know is God knows how you feel.
Some children are mean and cruel for no apparent reason.
You gotta believe in yourself this is the start of a new season.
Keep a positive attitude your nightmare is about to end.
Whatever you do you can't give up and you can't give in.
I know one thing people won't be laughing at you any more.
Once you become a business owner and a successful CEO.

2 Samuel 1:26 thy love to me was wonderful, that's God's love.
As a matter of fact God's love is more than I ever dreamed of.
You gotta have a dream and you gotta believe it will come true.
You gotta believe in yourself even if nobody else believes in you.
God can handle all you problems like stepping on a roach.
I'm here to encourage you and cheer you on like a football coach.
The Lord handles all of my problems like an exterminator.
By the way have you thought about being a private investigator?
You gotta believe in yourself you can be a weapons inspector.
You can be a body guard I think you'll be a good protector.
Help others don't bully others and don't let any body bully you.
Don't watch others get bullied there's something you can do.
If you can't stop it please go tell someone make the first step.
You gotta ask yourself what if that was me afraid to ask for help.
Make yourself some goals you can be a public defender.
If you make plenty of money one day you'll be a big spender.
Believe in yourself one day you might wanna work with steel.
You can join the army then one day you'll be trained to kill.
If you're a little over weight then you should lose a layer.
Make a difference in your community by becoming the mayor.
Believe in yourself look in the mirror and find you inner strength.
Stay out of trouble you can grow up and become the president.
You must be real special if you feel like you are an outsider.
You can show your compassion by being a daycare provider.
If you like animals then you can work with animal control.
Don't ever let anyone make you put your dreams on hold.

1 Kings 2:4 the Lord may continue his word he spoke concerning me.
You gotta read God's word it will enlighten you and set you free.
It's time for you to experience God's love and know that he's real.
Here's something for you to remember empathy is a learned skill.
You'll gain empathy if you try to imagine another person's plight.
You become a winner when you learn to walk away from a fight.
It might not be possible to feel someone else's pain completely.
I'm a winner because I refuse to let the devil win or defeat me.
A bully can't be a bully if no one is bothered or afraid of him.
A lot of people are blind to the fact that bullies have a problem.
What bullies do ain't right oh yah that's right that's for sure.
It's really a shame what innocent little kids have to endure.
I wish I could just snap my fingers and make it all go away.
I know I'll make a difference if I just take a few minutes to pray.
People get off when they see the pain of someone crying.
I'd like to see the wonderful design that you could be designing.
If you're the bully please stop right now before things go too far.
Somebody already loves you for the person you already are.
Don't sacrifice someone's feels to make someone laugh and smile.
I know what it feels like to be desperate and lonely as a child.
Let bygones be bygones everyone can't do what you can do.
Believe in yourself and look in the mirror and be true.
A tree sheds leaves in the fall, but in the spring they grow.
It's a way your can feel good without making others feel low.
Release your anger without being a bully or using your fist.
Pursue your dreams your encounter with God will give you bliss.

2 kings 4:9 I perceive that this is a holy man of God.
We can accomplish our dreams if we try nothing is too hard.
Some people call real miracles from God good luck or a fluke.
The devil makes me so mad sometimes he makes me puke.
You gotta concentrate on your goals you can be a game creator.
A bully is a small minded person nothing more then a hater.
If you live chemistry you can get a job working with the FDA.
Start making plans for the future now and you'll be okay.
You gotta believe in yourself you can be judge or a bank teller.
You can be a zoo keeper or you can build your own wine seller.
While you're in school you can earn money as a teller marketer.
But you can't stop there you deserve better you're a lot smarter.
Believe in yourself that's right I said it and you heard it from me.
Go after you dream you can be a hero or another great celebrity.
If you like driving why don't you consider being a truck driver?
I can see you now I bet you would be a phenomenal ski-diver.
If you learn to drive a truck you could get a job at Fed x.
You gotta believe in yourself and there's no telling what's next.
Don't let bullies change who you are you gotta be a peace maker.
You got your whole life ahead of you don't be a law breaker.
One day you might be a personal trainer or a make up artist.
People may hate you in your class because you're the smartest.
It's a reason you're smart I think you'll make a good spy.
One day you might find yourself working a case for the FBI.
Believe in yourself you can't lose hope not for one minute.
Find something you really like and put your whole heart in it.

1 Chronicles 29:13 we thank thee, and praise thy glorious name.
God is strong and mighty nobody can make me feel the same.
There are negative things that happened in the past you gotta let go.
Relationships have ended now it's time for you to move on and grow.
You gotta believe in yourself and the person you are now.
Sometimes you wanna move forward but you just don't know how.
Don't let the hurt you had in the past mess up your future plans.
I think you should try placing your life in God's hands.
It's hard enough trying to live, but you don't have to do it alone.
Everything was going well now you can't figure out what's wrong.
You gotta deal with life in the midst of the struggle and grief.
Unfortunately it's a shame all you gotta do is ask God for relief.
A bully can't bother you if you take the bullies power away.
Believe in yourself don't let the bully spoil another beautiful day.
Start thinking about whom you are and whom you wanna be.
You gotta believe in yourself and you gotta find your identity.
You can't let someone's action define the person you are.
If someone is invading your space don't let it go too far.
Don't let things get worst or wait for the other shoe to drop.
If someone is bullying you in anyway tell someone it has to stop.
People say sticks and stones break bones but words don't hurt.
I know personally words can really make you feel like dirt.
It's not good to keep all those feeling held up inside you.
Sometimes you really feel like there's nothing you can do.
Its bad enough you're still trying to see what life is about.
Now you got a bunch of problems that you can't figure out.

Believe in Yourself

2 Chronicles 1:12 wisdom and knowledge is granted unto thee.
The Lord gave riches and wealth and honor unto me.
I don't need to put someone down to give you a compliment.
I come to encourage you with hope I come to give you strength.
The Lord always gives me what I need more then I could expect.
Believe in yourself I see you being phenomenal very artistic.
Don't let people steal your joy and tare down your banner.
You gotta special eye I believe you'll be a good wedding planner.
You're special everybody can see it because it's a no brainer.
You got enough spunk to be a once in a life time physically trainer.
Those that like to read will be a great exceptional librarian.
Those that like animal they would make a great veterinarian.
I don't think you should settle for being a maid be, a therapist.
Get a piece of paper write down your goals make a list.
Years from now people that made fun of you will look like a fool.
One day you'll end up being a principle all a really good school.
It will be a really nice school because you will be there.
It would be real nice to see you doing your own T.V. repair.
You can do so many amazing things believe in yourself! Okay.
Your life would be so much better if you would learn to pray.
If you like to make people laugh don't be a bully be a comedian.
If you like killing people's dreams you should be a mortician.
I said that because you can't kill something that is already dead.
Don't hold you're head down hold you're head up look ahead.
Practice smiling one day you'll make a real good office clerk.
When you become the CEO you still gotta do a little office work.

Ezra 10:4 Arise; for this matter belongeth unto thee.
Be of good courage your problems don't belong to you or me.
God allows us to experience low points in life to teach us a lesson.
You gotta believe in yourself and then you gotta stop stressing.
Friends become bullies when they make rude comments to you.
Don't feel trapped it's time to move on and find someone new.
If you let people walk all over you they will do it from now on.
It's time for you to realize when people are treating you wrong.
Don't listen to people that call you dumb or call you stupid.
Some people can say rude things off the top of their head.
You gotta look in the mirror and learn to love what you see.
Be who you are believe in yourself be who you wanna be.
Live your life to the fullest; don't let one more day pass you by.
Don't hang around people that make you sad and make you cry.
Live your life be happy you're unique you have you're on style.
Believe in yourself and whatever you do learn to live and smile.
Dream big and believe in yourself it takes courage to dream.
If your friends don't play fare don't let them play on your team.
You gotta live your life now don't let no one give you a label.
It's time for you to bring all your hopes and dreams to the table.
Say goodbye to the people that can't see what's in your heart.
Don't waste you time hanging with people that tares you apart.
We can't choose our parents but we gotta love them anyway.
Stop hanging around people that don't had anything nice to say.
The way I see it they are blessed to be able to hang around you.
Believe in yourself and start being happy in everything you do.

Believe in Yourself

Nehemiah 1:6 let thine ear now be attentive.
When you confess your sin to the Lord he will forgive.
Everyone won't be receptive to your needs and who you are.
Believe in yourself you already know you was born a star.
Don't sale yourself short one day you'll be your own boss.
Jesus loves you he hung between two thieves on the cross.
If you believe in yourself it's time for you to believe in Jesus.
One thief asked Jesus If you're the Christ save yourself and us.
Jesus was receptive to those that were receptive to him.
Jesus is called the light because he shows up when hope is dim.
Life is a journey when life knocks you down you gotta fight.
People will push you into darkness but you gotta turn on the light.
Once you become a woman that means you're no longer a girl.
You gotta believe in yourself and find your place in the world.
Once you become a man that means you're no longer a boy.
You gotta believe in yourself and don't let no one steal your joy.
You're headed somewhere when you get in the car and drive.
Look deep inside yourself and make your dreams come alive.
Talk to someone before you're feelings make you explode.
Find someone you can talk to and share your heavy load.
You keep smiling when you're heart is filled with so much pain.
No one wants to make a difference but their quick to complain.
I learned a long time ago what goes up must come down.
When you go too far sometimes you gotta turn back around.
You can't keep on going when you know you done went too far.
Don't ever give up and don't ever be a shame of who you are.

Esther 7:2 what is thy petition queen ester and it shall be granted.
Ester found favor with the Lord from the seed's she planted.
Successful people don't give up they try different approaches.
Most coaches believe in his players and the team he coaches.
A good coach will push you to your full potential far as you can go.
Once you achieve one goal you gotta continue and do much more.
If things don't work out as planned you can't give up disappointed.
You gotta obtain the outcome and the results you wanted.
Don't be the one to give up and miss out on a chance at victory.
I'm a vey successful person and positive thinking did it for me.
You can't stop trying that will cause failure that's a guarantee.
You'll be successful believe in yourself be what you wanna be.
Don't be so hard on yourself because you will make mistakes.
You know what won't work start over give yourself a few breaks.
People give evaluations based on your behavior and your attitude.
Failure is a judgment from others but what does it really conclude.
Look at failure as a learning experience it's only a learning process.
Don't allow the fear of failing stop you from obtaining success.
You gotta believe in yourself it's time for you to start investing.
People can see your abilities and that's why they start protesting.
When people pull you down their protesting what they see in you.
People will try to stop you from seeing your dreams through.
The devil uses people to do his dirty work and get the job done.
When I see certain people coming believe me I get up and run.
I'm not afraid of them it's because I know which battles to fight.
I don't have to prove someone wrong just to prove I'm right.

Believe in Yourself

Job 37:14 stand, still and consider the wondrous words of God.
It's time to let the Lord heal you and restore your heart.
You are an eagle rise above your battle it's time for you to soar.
Don't let small minded people steal your peace and joy any more.
If you're the bully don't build yourself up by putting others down.
It's not too late for you to change and turn your life around.
Are you bullying others because you feel a little bit insecure?
Do you want others to feel some of the pain you had to endure?
I wanna encourage you to let all of that pain out and break free.
Talk to someone I bet you'll feel much better it's a guarantee.
Your time is too valuable to waste it so stop being distracted.
Some people will never apologize for the way they acted.
Words are powerful that can hurt you down in your soul.
If you don't forgive those that hurt you they maintain control.
Somebody will always spread rumors to make you look bad.
When those rumors aren't true it can really make you mad.
And some rumors hurt so bad they are really hard to ignore.
Don't let it rob your hope for tomorrow you can't cry no more.
Everyone has dream some have hopes of being a minor.
I love those that have an eye for being a clothes designer.
Some people love skinning animals just to get some fur.
Some people like to read they'll make a good book editor.
It's time for you to have some fun get out and play some golf.
You can represent Christ by being a man or woman of the cloth.
You can open a coffee shop or you can be a coffee importer.
You like to talk a lot so I think you'll be a real good reporter.

Psalm 18:2 the Lord is my rock and my fortress and my deliverer.
I'm not perfect I make mistakes I'm glad the Lord is a forgiver.
The devil use people to hurt one another and cause pain.
If you're not part of the solution don't you dare complain?
People will do things that can make you lose your mind.
Then you have to make a choice once they cross that line.
People will take your pain and make it their personal gain.
Consequences don't mean a thing to them nor does your pain.
Don't let people walk all over you don't let them make you cry.
Don't let anyone cause you unnecessary pain and ride it dry.
People try to make themselves look good to their own greed.
They don't care about your feelings or what you might need.
You need to avoid friends that always get you in trouble.
Whatever you lose in life God will give it back to you double.
Life is too short to be wasted you need to stop and evaluate.
Stop wasting time make use of your time before it is too late.
Be careful of the company you keep the people that hang with you.
Somehow they can change who you are by the things they do.
We take in information from the people we hand around.
If you can't change things don't let others bring you down.
We try to fit in to that world around us and I find that strange.
I was in that type of situation before and I had to change.
People can be a great influence in your life good or bad.
People think it's normal to hold a grudge and stay mad.
It's even more common that they want others to pick a side.
What would Jesus do in this case? Where is your pride?

Believe in Yourself

Proverbs 3:5 trust in the Lord with all thine heart.

Lean not unto thine own understanding whatever you do trust God.

When someone treats you bad don't get mad rejoice.

The Lord will be thrilled by your actions and your choice.

We are Christ like this is why they call us Christians.

We're sisters and brothers we are more than friends.

Ask yourself what would Jesus do and do what is right.

Make sure you do what you think Jesus would have done.

I'm only one person but I'm ready to praise God and have fun.

I can't do everything but I'll do something whatever I can.

It's nice to go to church on Sunday do you have a plan?

Don't leave the message at church that message was for you.

Believe in yourself you better get started you got work to do.

You can be a model can you sing can you hit a high note?

Maybe one day you can sing some of the songs I wrote.

The world is going to hate us for being Christians nowadays.

People will hate us more especially when we give God praise.

God's love will teach us how to forgive and help us forget.

Not what you see but what you feel and the pain you live with.

God's love will help you listen and help you understand.

If I see you crawling I wanna give you a helping hand.

God's love will help you let go and teach you how to hold on.

Stop being depressed believe in yourself stand up be strong.

You can climb any mountain one step at a time step by step.

Believe in yourself and don't ever be afraid to ask for help.

You can accomplish anything if you find the courage to try.

I want you to believe in yourself never let your dreams die.

Pastor Deborah Wofford

Ecclesiastes 3:1 to every thing there is a season.
A time to love and a time to hate everything happen for a reason.
I'm selfish with my salvation I love the Lord I won't sacrifice mine.
I'll help you obtain your salvation if you're willing to cross that line.
Are you ready to jump start your life with motivation and hope?
Don't let any one enter your space and make it impossible to cope.
Stand up for yourself tell someone if someone is bothering you.
Pain will eventually block your focus it will surely block your view.
I wanna build your Self Esteem I would lose just to let you win.
I would move your mountains so all your troubles will end.
I use poetry to express the beautiful of life without envy and pride.
Poetry is the tool I use to express how I feel deep down inside.
Believe in yourself you gotta be persistent until you finally succeed.
Let your heart be driven by love not material things or greed.
Don't even consider defeat remove it from your vocabulary right away.
Don't use any words or phrases that mean failure as of today.
Don't ever quit or say you can't it's out of the question for now.
It's impossible for you to lose because you don't know how.
Believe in yourself starting today as of now you are unable to fail.
Failure is not an option for you any more as far as I can tell.
Any one that thinks you're hopeless must be some kind of fool.
Believe in yourself because I truly believe you're really cool.
Your life has purpose you're the owner of a new attitude.
Day by day positive thoughts will give you hope and gratitude.
I'm giving you empowerment I'm firmly promoting hope and success.
Believe in yourself your life as a purpose with no need for stress.

Songs of Solomon 1:2 for thy love is better than wine.
I'm so glad the Lord loves me and his heart is mine.
At the age of 33 Jesus was condemned to death on the cross.
He paid for our sins he died so our souls wouldn't be lost.
Jesus was a perfect man he did nothing wrong yet he died.
Only the worst criminals were condemned to be crucified.
Jesus was nailed to the cross by His hands and feet.
Each nail was 6 to 8 inches long Jesus came to defeat.
The nails were driven into His wrist it had to hurt pretty badly.
When I think of his death on the cross it really saddens me.
Jesus had to be in pain both of His feet were nailed together.
The thought of his death makes me wanna live so much better.
Imagine the struggle, pain, suffering, and the courage he had.
Jesus endured this reality for over 3 hours he never got mad.
A few minutes before He died, Jesus stopped bleeding.
As the tears ran down my face I cried I had to stop reading.
Jesus endured this experience to open the Gates of Heaven.
We oughta worship him with all our heart twenty four seven.
Jesus died so that you and I could have free access to God.
Your sins will be washed away and you'll have a clean heart.
Don't be ashamed to share the good news Jesus died for you.
Don't be worried about what others may say, think, or do.
Tell all your friends what Jesus experienced to save us all.
You gotta appreciate God's power and the blessings that fall.
God is the source of my strength my Savior and my friend.
He keeps me focused day and night he made my troubles end.

Isaiah 51:15 but I am the Lord thy God that divided the sea.
The Lord will do something miraculous like that for you and me.
The darkness may fill your life but God provides you enough light.
You know a new day is approaching once the clock hits midnight.
Life has an order in which different events and changes take place.
God will teach you how to deal with life with a smile on your face.
Happy events bring joy when life is good you're happy and glad.
Traumatic events often leave you feeling hopeless and pretty sad.
Without encouragement life has a way of making you lose sight.
Life traps you in a dark places I give hope by giving spiritual light.
I provide knowledge and the proof you need to make a firm decision.
I plant seeds by helping you find your journey and your vision.
We are the body of Christ we gotta look out for each other's distress.
You can't see behind you but I can see the spot on your suit or dress.
The Lord expects us to look out for each other in a sweet manner.
We're can't hold anyone's faults against them by hanging up a banner.
The Lord expects us to have compassion on our sister and brothers.
We gotta learn to look out for people we gotta love and help others.
I can't stop the rain from falling but I'll dry you off it you get wet.
I'll help you make choices that won't leave you with regret.
If you walk in my shoes follow the good foot steps not my bad choices.
The Lord pays close attention to a heart that's sincere and rejoices.
The way you live today will affect the outcome of your tomorrow.
Believe in yourself don't live with regret and a heart of sorrow.
Live your life with courage you gotta have fun life is a blast.
Don't forget what you have today may very well be gone in a flash.

Believe in Yourself

Jeremiah 29:11 I know the thoughts that I think towards you my friend.
God has thoughts of peace not of evil to give you an expected end.
Believe in yourself every thought you have is a dream come true.
What you accomplish or obtain in life all depends up to you.
You can be a counselor or you can settle for being a butler.
Just because a woman carries a child doesn't mean she's a mother.
Believe in yourself when I was young curiosity was hard to resist.
If you like science you may be headed towards being a pharmacist.
A career is started with thoughts ideas and a few suggestions first.
Something's you will be great with and something's you'll be worst.
If you like flying kites you may wanna be a pilot on a plane.
You'll be a good doctor if you have compassion for people in pain.
Be a dentist and teach people the values of keeping their teeth clean.
You can teach the world what the word of God really mean.
Believe in yourself if you like to travel you can work on the rail road.
Use you're free time having fun like riding a bike or a skate board.
I know a lot of teens can't wait until their old enough to work.
Most teens start out at restaurants they start out being a sales clerk.
You get to see how some people live if you were a house keeper.
Once you start paying bills you learn to live a little bit cheaper.
Some people take pride in being a foster parent to those in need.
Some people do it for the money with a heart full of greed.
Well someone has to be a superintendant and a mail man.
You can be a professional boxer it takes hard work and a plan.
Believe in yourself you can be a famer or the captain on a ship.
You might have yourself a little fun riding a horse with a whip.

Lamentations 3:25 the Lord is good unto them that wait for him.
Be patient what on the Lord he will handle your problem.
You're moving into God's glory you're life won't be the same.
Whatever you lay your hands upon shall prosper in Jesus name.
Your dream will not die your plans won't fail you will succeed.
Your destiny won't be aborted you'll get everything you need.
The desires of your heart will be granted it's headed your way.
Your mess is now your miracle and your message as of today.
Money will know your name and address from this day forward.
Your maximum will become your minimum if you trust the Lord.
People will bother you when it's time for another blessing.
Heaven already confirmed it hold your head up stop stressing.
This is the ending of your sufferings no more sorrows and pain.
The Lord is about to bless you his love will shower you like rain.
He that sits on the throne has remembered your name today.
God removed all your hardship peace and joy is on the way.
The Lord will never let you down remember he loves you.
The Lord will leave you in awe with the wonderful things he do.
Bullies are intimidated by you because you're wonderful and smart.
Don't let nobody make you carry anger and hate in your heart.
I can put on a fake smile better than jewelry and make up.
I love the Lord if it wasn't for him my heart would be corrupt.
I use to smile so the pain in my heart wouldn't cover by face.
I have a real smile now since God decided to show me grace.
It's only a matter of time before your enemies are taken down.
The Lord's mighty right hand can turn you whole life around.

Ezekiel 7:8 now will I shortly pour out my fury upon thee.
The Lord will take vengeance upon those that envy me.
God has placed favor on my ministry he carries me far and wide.
I openly share the pain I carried around for years trying to hide.
I share the gospel and my miraculous testimony everywhere.
I share my testimony to help remove other people's despair.
Every opportunity I get I bravely step up to the microphone.
People need to know Jesus is a healer the one I depend on.
Jesus is a Savior he's my deliverer and a phenomenal friend.
It's a joy to serve the Lord and a greater joy to be born again.
I've had a lot of rejection a lot of people laugh and turn me down.
People aren't ready to hear how Jesus turned my life around.
The congregation ain't quit ready for a testimony like mine.
People back away once I tell them how I crossed that line.
My testimony is an inspiration to others here and there.
Through my gift of poetry I've touch people everywhere.
God has given me many other gifts to help me lift up his name.
Once you've been healed physically you'll never be the same.
Spiritual healing is the greatest gift God ever gave me.
Financially God made it possible for me to live debt free.
I'm mentally standing in the middle of a major breakthrough.
The Lord smiled when I humbly tried something new.
Take a moment to view your life right now where you are.
I want others to see exactly how the Lord brought me this far.
I find myself having my own private workshop and revival.
I don't need a crusade or a special event I only need my bible.

Daniel 9:4 I prayed unto the Lord my God and made my confession.
I believe the Lord will forgive me for my transgression.
Bullies can take so much out of you but you can be restored.
I've seen gang members and drug addicts turn to the Lord.
You can face the future by standing up for yourself today.
You'll have confidence for every situation you face along the way.
Don't let a bully rob you of your Self Esteem and your identity.
Turn to the Lord in your distress He'll take care of your enemy.
Live your dream your future is filled with promises from the Lord.
Believe in yourself do your best and continue to move forward.
Start exercising and let some of that anger and frustration out.
Get yourself back on your journey you gotta get on the right route.
Go into the world uncorrupted I walk with God come walk beside me.
Take a breath of fresh air in this squalid and polluted society.
Provide people with a glimpse of good life and the God we serve.
Stop letting other people control you by getting on your nerve.
I know what it is to be in need, and I know what it is to have plenty.
I'm well fed I'm not hungry because the Lord my God lives in me.
I have learned the secret of being content in every situation I face.
Because I made it this far skating on my heavenly father's grace.
When we let our own light shine others can see the Lord.
We consciously give others a glimpse of their eternal reward.
Liberated from our own fear we can help liberate others.
I automatically have great compassion for single mothers.

Hosea 14:4 I will heal their backsliding I will love them freely.
I felt like the Lord was pacifically directing that at me.
I wanna assist you in finding inner peace and your dream.
From this moment on I'm rooting for you I'm on your team.
At this moment you gotta begin chasing your dreams down.
Nothing people say can discourage you or turn you around.
Your life is important and your happiness means a lot to me.
Today is the day you gotta concentrate on breaking free.
Don't let anything holding you down and knock you off track.
You're moving into your destiny can't nothing hold you back.
You gotta future since God forgave all your transgressions.
Life is about love not about material things and possessions.
People work tirelessly for the things they accumulate.
None of it means anything if you constantly surrounded by hate.
People can take you back to places that once caused you pain.
People don't know that your peace is real hard to maintain.
Everything I had or use to own in my life no longer matter.
I climbed my way out of my rut using the bible as my latter.
The Lord became my, everything and he remains my all.
The past was a struggle because I would constantly fall.
Once the pain and heartache was gone I stop isolating and crying.
The overwhelming sadness stopped me from living and trying.
Everything I lost continues to surpass everything I've gained.
God gave me the courage to go after everything I've obtained.
The Lord changed my whole life and gave me my heart's desire.
God directed me as I pursued my dreams down to the last wire.

Joel 2:21 be glad and rejoice for the Lord will do great things.
The Lord will take care of you just like a bumble bee stings.
God's goodness and fullness came in handy in the after math.
I gotta share God's word with everyone that enters my path.
My faith dares me to be all that the Lord called me to be.
My challenges gave me the courage to help others break free.
It's evident that I encourage you to believe in yourself.
You gotta fix your own life stop worrying about everyone else.
You gotta figure out what puts the sunshine in each day.
Try to figure out how to trust God and he will make a way.
I've seen glimpses of hope for the future and that goes for you.
You gotta believe in yourself and see your dreams through.
I know you're getting tired of those emerging fears you face.
Don't let anyone dictator failure upon you or enter your space.
Fear is destroying the good that you carry deep down inside.
Don't let your healthy habits die because of the pain you hide.
Believe in yourself and watch the things that hurt you disappear.
Education is important you'll make accomplishments without fear.
People try to control undesirable people by degrading them.
Jesus is real but people don't wanna openly talk about him.
Horrific crimes are committed by bullies starting at an early age.
Nobody pays attention to all the clear signs of hate and rage.
Punishable behaviors are ignored and unconsciously rewarded.
When people make excused for someone the truth is distorted.
Believe in yourself and give yourself love and satisfaction.
When something needs to be done be bold enough to take action.

Believe in Yourself

Amos 5:6-seek the Lord and ye shall live; that's what the word said.
Believe in yourself and follow the Lord on the journey ahead.
Belief is very vital either you believe in yourself or you don't.
You can argue with me or believe me and go after what you want.
I can't rebel against God and expect all my needs to be met.
Sin will separate me from God and ultimately leave me with regret.
My relationship with the Lord requires me to serve him in deed.
In return the Lord promised me he would supply my every need.
God choose me at this point to carry out my assignment.
My actions and my deeds must constantly be in perfect alignment.
God wants you to believe in yourself because he believes in you.
The Lord will show you what's real and what isn't true.
Believe in yourself but must of all believe in the word of God.
Believing in God is what will sustain you when life gets hard.
It's not about believing in your own ability its God's power in you.
Belief is the psychological state in which cause a breakthrough.
Faith is the foundation of our way of thinking and believing.
Perception is our method of thinking hope is what we're receiving.
In normal life we don't question our own behavior and belief.
Once we change our way of thinking we can release our grief.
People form an opinion of others based on our actions and attitude.
Our attitude is how we act or react it's the volume of our mood.
Usually we don't see our own action except in front of the mirror.
It was a child trapped inside of me and no one could hear her.
Don't make the same mistake speak up let your voice be heard.
No one understood me but I found solace in God's holy word.

Pastor Deborah Wofford

Obadiah 1:3 the pride of thine heart hath deceived thee.
Life can fool us at times and we find ourselves trying to break free.
Your actions are off balanced when you do drugs or drink.
The way we act is directly influenced by the way we think.
Some people already know what the Lord wants them to do.
Listen to the Lord he has a few instructions concerning you.
Your values can never compare to the values the Lord see.
The Lord knows exactly who you are and who you can be.
Imma introduce you to God's word in a sweet and nice tone.
You gotta believe in yourself and leave that sweet comfort zone.
Don't stick with the old way of thinking and what you use to do.
Examine yourself trust God he has a wonderful plan for you.
Don't blame God for all the pain you suffered or had to endure.
The Lord is full of compassion his love is tender and pure.
Believe in yourself move forward don't be stagnant any more.
It's time to identify your dreams and see what God has in store.
People that are fooled by the devil are a menace to society.
Terror comes in many different forms it comes in a variety.
How you handle life's trials speaks volumes to who you are.
People that break real easy usually don't make it that far.
Don't be someone you're not or what others want you to be.
You gotta look in the mirror and be proud of what you see.
Don't feel like you gotta act differently in order to fit in.
Teens face this problem everyday as their characters begin.
Stop trying to be more popular trying to please the crowd.
Believe in yourself look in the mirror and just be proud.

Believe in Yourself

Jonah 1:17 Jonah was in the belly of the fish 3 days & 3 nights.
Can you imagine being trapped with no foods and no lights?
Some bargains are simply bargains sent straight from hell.
Some people will set you up just to sit and watch you fail.
That pursuit of happiness and friendship leads no where.
Next time you see those type of friends leave them right there.
Look at your own behavior and see if you really fit in.
Pay close attention to the people you consider your friend.
Gossip is terrible it hurts and it makes other people feel bad.
Once someone's feelings get hurt someone winds up mad.
Gossip is the product of many bad habits people obtain.
As people run out of things to say they gossip and complain.
Some people talk about the mistakes other people made?
Then they act like they won every game they played.
Believe in yourself because you are one of a kind.
Don't cross over into the darkness don't ever cross that line.
Certain people will entice you to go down the wrong road.
Sometimes you gotta stop and ask God to carry your load.
Sometimes you can make a mistake and be doomed for life.
Your everlasting punishment is living in misery and strife.
People do evil things then they say God sent them your way.
I want you to be able to notice evil spirits and learn to pray.
You gotta be able to forgive people without thinking twice.
I gotta focus on pleasing my Lord and savior Jesus Christ.
You don't need friends that move you further from your goals.
Get away from evil people and grab life and all that it holds.

Micah 7:7 I will wait for the God of my salvation my God will hear me.
Don't try to get even with anyone let the Lord handle your enemy.
Whatever your goal in life is your friends should support it.
Friends should motivate you and encourage you not to quit.
Hanging with the wrong crowd will cause you to lose track.
Once you lose time it's gone forever you can't get it back.
It's time to be a spontaneous start exciting your freedom in Christ.
Live your live believe in yourself remember we don't live twice.
Promiscuity is like cancer is spreads it's far from my mind.
I can't live destructively I gotta be loving, sweet and kind.
The Holy Spirit will travel through your mind, body and soul.
The Holy Spirit form emotional bonds we can't control.
The Lord divides is love among us with all fairness in mine.
The mind instills fear and guilt to keep us distorted and blind.
Sometimes we feel ourselves trapped in our own insecurities.
Whatever hardens our heart will cause us to fall to our knees.
I wanna make God proud and live my life the way God intend.
I trust the Lord I'm no longer that girl that plays pretend.
What ever you can't fix let God use his platform to get it done.
Whatever we think is impossible God said it's a victory won.
Let God use his platform on your behalf to display his glory.
Use the word of God and apply it to your life don't worry.
People use a stealthy way to worm their way into your heart.
We try to find the good in people then we let down our guard.
We get weak from time to time then we get burdened with sin.
We make promises and break them over and over again.

Believe in Yourself

Nahum 1:3 the Lord is slow to anger and great in power.
The Lord is with you he protects you every second of the hour.
The Lord is ready to change your life his love is renown.
The power of the Lord is spectacular it has never let me down.
I never been homeless but I found myself facing destitute.
I was impulsive until God said I can rest once I tell the truth.
I love David he sinned and he still was willing to tell his story.
Israel went through one of their driest seasons in history.
God will speak to you because He's sensitive to the subject.
Pay attention when the Lord speaks don't be left with regret.
The Lord's plans for your life are simply extraordinary.
The just shall live by faith especially when times get scary.
Sight and focus are very crucial in accessing God's blessings.
Your dreams will come true once you stop stressing.
Stop focusing on the things you can see with your eyes.
Keep your eyes focused on God he made the beautiful skies.
People can't see the spirit realm they focus on what they see.
If you move by sight you faith isn't where it supposes to be.
With ordinary faith you're limited to the thing you receive.
Don't down play your faith based on the things you believe.
You gotta stop listening to what's happening around you.
The economy is bad but you gotta expect a breakthrough.
The Lord will open your heart and He'll open your ears.
Let the Lord take away your sadness and your fears.
You be able to see the invincible when God opens your eyes.
You'll be speechless when the Lord catches you by surprise.

Habakkuk 2:2 write; the vision and make it plain upon tables.
Believe in yourself trust God and don't be fooled by labels.
Your vision is your dreams the Lord said write it down.
The plans the Lord has for you are extra ordinary and profound.
Life has a way of making us carry some real heavy loads.
Then we end up traveling down some real lonely roads.
I can still remember the day the Lord became my friend.
The Lord always stuck by me through thick and thin.
The day I found the Lord I found true love and affection.
Even though I sin the Lord has never made me feel rejection.
The Lord is the only one that can feel the emptiness inside.
I don't have to feel a shame of the thing I tried to hide.
I was headed straight to hell I was on the wrong route.
God's amazing grace carried me and brought me out.
God gave me so much peace that I have hope for tomorrow.
I was sleeping when the Lord came and took away my sorrow.
The day I found Jesus is the day I found the love I was after.
The Lord filled my heart with joy I feel peace and laughter.
I'm grateful I gotta love that's unconditional and it's all mine.
God's love is unexplainable is sweet most of all its divine.
A good friend will never let you go through things alone.
God knows how to take the blues away and fix what's wrong.
Remember success is acquired through following Gods plan.
Don't let pride stop you from doing the best you can.
Whatever goes up will eventually come back down.
Peace and happiness will always follow you around.

Zephaniah 1:14 the great day of the Lord is near; He's coming back.
Remember you are special that's why the devil chose you to attack.
Let God have the Glory for all He continues to do in our lives.
We gotta give him glory for all He gives and all He provides.
I urge you to remain firm in upholding the things of God.
I don't know everything but I know I'm after God's heart.
Violent situation destructiveness and danger is all around us.
If you're in danger or trouble call on the Lord Jesus.
You can scream and shout to the Lord with a thankful heart.
Whatever is holding you back you oughta turn it over to God.
We got different backgrounds and we got different techniques.
Whatever is in your heart that's what you're mouth speaks.
People use others to express their anger like a punching bag.
After a bully hurt someone they go sit around and they brag.
The victim is left trying to find the means of survival.
Everything the victim need is in the 66 books of the bible.
The bible gives you tools to help you along with God's grace.
Stop focusing on the situation that you were forced to face.
The bible give you hope when everything else is about to fade.
The Lord will let you learn from the mistakes you made.
You'll remember the people in the bible that told their story.
The bible tells how tribulations caused God to get the glory.
Don't believe in magic and don't let anyone poison your soul.
Violent people will make you feel like they are in control.
Then your pain feels bigger then life and continues to grow.
The peace of almighty God will sustain you like never before.

Haggai 2:7 I will fill this house with glory saith the Lord of host.
I love the Lord He anointed me and gave me the Holy Ghost.
We gotta pray for each other to overcome these wicked days.
We gotta stop complaining and give God's some high praise.
Prayer is how we communication with God on any level.
We gotta stay close to God and He'll protect us from the devil.
God's thoughts aren't our own his thoughts are much higher.
God designed you He's gonnta give you you're hearts desire.
The Lord bestowed his love and all his blessings upon you.
God shows you how much he loves you by the things he do.
Starting with, giving his only son the greatest man in history.
The bible inspires me the Lord and his wonderful story.
He didn't have any servants but he was called master.
The thought of his love makes my heart beat so much faster.
Jesus didn't have a degree but they called him teacher.
When he spoke everyone listened so I call him a preacher.
He didn't have any medicine but they called him healer.
He sat with robbers, thieves he even sat with a killer.
He didn't have an army but he made the devil's head swirl.
He didn't win any military battles but he conquered the world.
The Lord never committed any crimes but they crucified Him.
Every where Jesus went he healed and solved every problem.
They crucified my Jesus and then they buried him in a tomb.
But the Lord still lives to this day I feel his spirit in this room.
Jesus lives in me I'm here to make sure his name is glorified.
Jesus deserves our praise after all he endured before he died.

Believe in Yourself

Zechariah 14:9 and the Lord shall be King over all the earth.
The Lord Jesus was announced the king way before his birth.
God gave Jesus a name that caused all the demons to tremble.
When I look in the mirror there's no question of who I resemble.
I am my father's daughter and I know he loves me very much.
I inherited my heart's desire once I felt the Lord's holy touch.
Imma wait on the Lord in the shadows posted up by the wall.
My mind is set on Jesus my needs are met with just one call.
The Lord hides me from searching evil eyes all day long.
When the evening twilights come I won't fear I'm never alone.
I watch the clouds part because the moon is giving me light.
I love God I respect others and I take care of my loved ones.
I try to make the children of our future put down those guns.
I serve the Lord with compassion I cater to him with respect.
Before I finish the first assignment I look for the next project.
I notice whenever I'm not afraid to fail I don't I succeed.
I'll stay focused and prepare myself with everything I need.
I live my life to the fullest I take the necessary steps to grow.
I trust the Lord and sometimes that requires me to lay low.
Sometimes I feel like the ground beneath me is about to fall.
I remind myself its ok and I continue to give God my all.
I just wanna remind you that the Lord really loves you.
All those that work on your nerve already have a clue.
You don't have to carry all those burdens alone any more.
Give Jesus your problems things won't be like they were before.
The Lord already knows your struggles and your pain.
God is ready to heal you and take that load off your brain.

Pastor Deborah Wofford

Malachi 3:12 and all nations shall call you blessed.
Jesus saved my life the day I called upon him and confessed.
God said you turned away when he looked you in the eye.
You didn't see him standing there when he watched you cry.
He said you hesitated when he asked you if you were alright.
God loves you he watches you with compassion day and night.
It seems like you're fighting for your life and you just won.
It's time for you to believe in yourself and have some fun.
You can stop feeling wide awake in your lonely nightmare.
God will show up on time he'll come from out of no where.
Every painful memory has its mark and a painful scar.
God want you to know he loves you just the way you are.
The Lord knows we get lost sometime and we lose our way.
When we get back up again he makes everything okay.
You gotta believe in yourself remember it's never too late.
It's time for you to follow your dreams don't procrastinate.
The devil is still acting up but that really doesn't surprise me.
When the Lord listens to my cries he makes me feel free.
I'm celebrating the Lord I hope my joy spread over there.
If you're heart is hurting I want you to know I really care.
Raising children nowadays can be like pulling a tooth.
I've learned that it's much easier if we tell them the truth.
It's ridiculous to make up stories that have no truth at all.
I believe that right there is setting them up to take a fall.
We oughta tell them the truth about the Lord Jesus Christ.
Instead of teaching them, girls are made of sugar and spice.

Matthew 5:8-Blessed are the pure in heart for they shall see God.
Remember God almighty is with you when life gets too hard.
You can't control others but you can control your own action.
If your life is unmanageable it may require a little subtraction.
You may need to erase a few things in order to get some peace.
If you subtract a few things maybe you'll get a little increase.
When you plant seeds in your garden you expect it to grow.
You gotta pick out the weeds to make it grow a little more.
Some people in life will hold you back and slow you down.
Before you know it you'll be completely turned around.
Instead of you being headed to college you'll be headed to jail.
Instead of you being on a route to heaven you'll be headed to hell.
God has a purpose for your life but you make things hard.
The difference between life and death is learning to obey God.
Successful people keep going no matter what other people say.
They take the good with the bad and let nothing stand in their way.
Life can turn out many different ways you gotta stay on your toes.
Just like one incident can have ninety nine different scenarios.
You must be aware of your actions and who your actions will affect.
You gotta believe in yourself and show others love and respect.
First you gotta love God and trust him enough to obey.
Your life will soar once you learn how to surrender and pray.
Let your heart be pure let go of your anger, malice and the hate.
Get rid of the things you can't digest that you got on your plate.
Don't let any body tie you up and put your soul in a knot.
You don't need people to make you try to be something you're not.

Mark 4:9 Jesus said he that hath ears to hear let him hear.
Once you obtain salvation with God he'll speak loud and clear.
Anger don't only hurt us it makes us hurt others people too.
Anger hurts others including people we love without a clue.
We need to find a healthy way to process our anger.
Maybe you can try bending and twisting a wire hanger.
God is gentle you'll hear him in your spirit when he speak.
Anger can take over you and make you some what weak.
People will push you're buttons just to make you angry.
I stay away from people that cause a lot of pain for me.
Once anger kicks in believe me it will stir up the devils nest.
Once the anger spreads it turns into a boat load of stress.
Anger is an emotion that is expressed with intimation and fear.
When you see someone angry you can believe the devil is near.
Anger causes people to do things that they normally wouldn't do.
The only one that is able to control your anger is you.
Don't let people change how you feel about yourself deep inside.
I was defined by my past until I decided to change the old me died.
People called me fat so I started saying it's more of me to love.
Once I started believing in myself my dreams was all I thought of.
A bully will stop bothering you once your anger stop showing.
If people say something mean just laugh and keep on going.
A bully is hyped up by the control he seems to have on someone.
Bullies will use other people as a laughing stock just to have fun.
On the other hand you gotta be clever by keeping your cool.
You gotta figure out how to make the bully look like the fool.

Believe in Yourself

Luke 11:3 Give-us day by day our daily bread.
That means hope and unconditional love for the road ahead.
Imma serve Christ and have a wonderful life with him.
I gotta serve Christ he gave me peace when my hope is dim.
I'm determined to fulfill the purpose the Lord has for me.
I'm determined to live with Christ when I get to glory.
I wanna make the Lord proud of me by my actions everyday.
I'm determined to make the Lord smile every time I pray.
I wanna help you obtain deliverance and inner healing.
I wanna help you obtain salvation if you're ready and willing.
It's time for Jesus to comfort you and shut the gates of hell.
I wanna prove to you God's unconditional love will never fail.
This year is the year to expect indescribable acts for every believer.
I'm a true worshipper because of Christ I'm a great achiever.
I love waiting in the presence of God waiting for Him to act.
I love laughing and smiling watching the Lord having my back.
I love looking in the mirror being myself expressing how I feel.
I don't feel the need to put on a front I really enjoy being real.
I'm fearless and I'm wonderfully made the Lord created me.
The Lord gave me a piece of his heart and made me hate free.
My family means a lot to me I gotta be an example everyday.
I gotta vision for those filled with pain and done lost their way.
God created in me a big heart to love and care for our nation.
God is pulling down strong holds to provide love and salvation.
The Lord wants to hold you in his arms and open a few doors.
The main thing you need to know is God loves you and he restores.

John 14:14-If ye shall ask anything in my name I will do it.
Believe in yourself learn to make choices you can live with.
Don't be depress over circumstances that God can solve for you?
God knows exactly how to bring you out an bring you through
You gotta let prayer and meditation lead you on your journey.
I meditate daily because I never know which way God will turn me.
Jesus said I can ask God for anything in him name and it's mine.
Lord will you lend me your eyes so I won't be spiritually blind.
There are so many different evil spirits that you and I can't see.
I'm so glad I have my sweet heavenly father looking after me.
I wish I was there to hug you and help you release your distress.
I'm praying for you I know the Lord will get you through this mess.
I know I can ask God for anything in his will and he'll give it to me.
My sweet loving father rewards me for the things I do for free.
A lot of children log on the World Wide Web every single day.
They are exposed to strangers that can harm them in someway.
Hidden among them are predators who navigate the cyber world.
They exploit social networking sites to find a sweet boy or girl.
They formed their own networks they trading tips with each other.
Lord I pray you stop that pain from being afflicted on a mother.
I know prayer works so I talk to the Lord and I know he will respond.
I love to pray I love spending time with the Lord so we can bond.
Imma pray I wanna make a difference before another child is hurt.
I pray that the Lord will stop bullies from treating others like dirt.
Please pray and join the fight against bullies it happens everyday.
You may feel like there's nothing you can do, but you can pray.

Acts 18:9—Be not afraid but speak and hold not thy peace.
Once you give your life to God he will make your joy increase.
You can accomplish anything with the right mind set.
First of all you gotta act like you and failure never met.
If people call you dumb it's because you're smarter than them.
Don't focus on the size of your trouble Jesus said focus on him.
Your mindset should be on winning and nothing less.
No matter what you do give your all and do your best.
Keep dreaming until you're heart takes it's last beat.
Don't ever give up stay positive don't ever accept defeat.
If you had a bucket you could catch some of the rain.
Every tear you cry will release some of your hideous pain.
You'll invent something that will be admired all across the world.
You can make something exquisite like a lamp made of pearl.
Believe in yourself you don't have to be famous to be rich.
You gotta learn how to present your ideas with a perfect pitch.
Make people think they are missing out on something great.
Learn to be spontaneous take chances don't procrastinate.
You gotta live your dream success is only a few steps away.
You gotta take a step closer to your destiny everyday.
No matter how high the water gets you won't drown.
No matter how bad things look God won't let you down.
Believe in yourself you'll catch up even if you're losing the race.
Your next in line for a miracle, God decided to show you grace.
If you touch one person's life you can touch many more.
Remember you're blessed if you got four walls and a floor.

Romans 12:21 be not overcome with evil overcome evil with good.
Listen to positive people and learn to live the way you should.
Being grateful will start God's favor his love will continue to stir.
The Lord will open your eyes when all you see is a blur.
Listen close you oughta stay in school so you can learn.
Build a relationship with God he'll show you which way to turn.
Believe in yourself follow your heart it's time for you to relax.
Prepare yourself for success take some time to get all the facts.
Look in the mirror and say to yourself "you were born to win"
Tell yourself that everyday and say it over and over again.
Your attitude has a lot to do with how far you will go.
Believe in yourself all your blessings will come in a row.
Every time you loose it's a setup for a comeback to win.
Success starts with the beginning the middle and the end.
You're headed for a miracle you're on the right road.
When you get tired of your baggage let God carry your load.
Stay strong it's only a matter of time before you succeed.
Don't be a follower you gotta learn how to take the lead.
Don't follow man you gotta follow Christ and follow him alone.
You're almost there keep going right don't do no wrong.
At this point your vision should be very clear in your head.
Thank God for everything you accomplish before you go to bed.
You gotta start each day with a big powerful step.
The Lord is standing by waiting for you to ask for help.
The day will come when you can shout victory forever more.
That victory will make you feel like you got a lot to live for.

Believe in Yourself

1 Corinthians 13:4 Love is patient and kind.

I heard a whole lot of people say that love is blind.

Always be ready to take a chance believe me it will come.

Thank God for everything that's where your blessings are from.

When you read your bible you need to say a prayer first.

Then you gotta look at the context or the subject of the verse.

The Lord talked about physical things like having a feast.

Jesus walked around everyday healing folks and offering peace.

The Lord talked about having wine and having a good time.

Things that take money Jesus made it happen without a dime.

Money answers many problems but it's not always the answer.

Money can't heal but the Lord can heal any type of cancer.

Some people don't believe or perceive how much God loves them.

The Lord don't love like the world does we gotta trust him.

Money can cause just as many problems as it couldda solved.

Every area of my life I invited the Lord Jesus to get involved.

You can't tell who a person is because they fellowship with you.

People in church will really surprise you by the things they do.

Some people get real happy over a nice glass of wine.

After one drink some people will go way across the line.

The Lord has taught me a lot and I learn a lot everyday.

Some times you gotta be patient and let God lead the way.

That was hard for me because I want things done right now.

What's really sad I tried to fix things when I didn't know how?

People profess Christianity but money is a god for them.

God said don't ever put anything or anyone before him.

2 Corinthians 4:8-We are troubled on every side yet not distressed.
No matter how many troubles you face you're still blessed.
We face trials everyday some are bigger then the rest.
Some days you get out of bed and everything seems to be a mess.
At that very moment we gotta stop for a minute and say a prayer.
Then we need to stand still and take a breath of fresh air.
On the other hand some trials are just a simply learning process.
We must face them head on and don't let it cause us any extra stress.
We need to deal with things in a manner that won't get us in trouble.
If we fly off the handle it will cause our existing problems to double.
Life is wonderful we gotta learn to deal with life's knock me down's.
I wanna be known for my bouncing back and my great rebound's.
I messed up so many times my own family through in the towel.
I wanted to make something out of my life but I didn't know how.
I have great determination if I start something I'll see it through.
Life can be overwhelming that's why I wanna encourage you.
Life may seem like a raw deal you have the power to change that.
Don't rush to get where you're going enjoying life where you're at.
Stop for a minute and look outside and just enjoy the view.
Make life interesting find a way to enjoy everything you do.
Don't let anyone push you all the way to the breaking point.
Don't let anyone cause you to have stress and pain in every join.
Exercise so you can free your mind and learn how to meditate.
Start ignoring people without it bothering you don't take the bait.
You gotta figure out a way to stay out of trouble and stay on top.
You gotta be strong it's time for you to make all the pain stop.

Believe in Yourself

Galatians 6:2-Bear one another's burdens & fulfill the law of Christ.
People will be jealous and talk about you if you're rude or nice.
You gotta believe the Blood of Jesus still works nowadays.
Remember strongholds break when you give God praise.
The blood of Jesus still has power his blood restores.
Don't you know the blood of Jesus open many doors?
Plead the Blood of Jesus over any situation you face.
The Lord is full of compassion he has unlimited grace.
Plead the blood over everything and watch things change.
Watch things come in your life that was out of your range.
You'll start seeing results according to the will of God.
You'll be able to obtain a new level of peace in you're heart.
Activate your faith in the blood of Jesus right now today.
The devil done stole your joy stop letting him get in the way.
The Lord created you he formed your inward parts perfectly.
He knitted you together in your mother's womb rather gently.
I thank God because he made you a picture perfect sight.
You're a wonderful unique person the Lord made you just right.
It's time for you to be fearless and hold your head up straight.
You were wonderfully made and that's not up for debate.
The Lord made you with high quality and high definition.
You'll have a better self-image if you see yourself the way God do.
Believe in yourself don't let anyone change your opinion of you.
Look in the mirror smile it's time for your Self Esteem to elevate.
Stop lowering your standards get up and stand up straight!
Stand firm with the quality of life you had before Satan's lies!
Look in the mirror and enjoy the reflection of your own eyes.

Ephesians 6:11 Put on the whole armour of God a new level.
So you will be able to stand against the wiles of the devil.
I'm totally devoted to God I abide in him and he abides in me.
I enjoy sharing the pure joy of the Lord's love and intimacy.
Imma abide in his word simply because I'm in love with Christ.
Imma remain in the Lord's presence for me it's not a sacrifice.
Imma continue representing my Lord and sweet savior Jesus.
The Lord wants to pass his love on to others through us.
A child of God is led by the Spirit like a child in his youth.
A child of God must worship the Father in Spirit and in truth.
One that isn't free from sin but free from any kind of jealousy.
We can't hold bitterness and we can't rebel against thee.
A child of God can't have un-forgiveness in their heart.
Imma worship the Lord in spirit and in truth it's not that hard.
I asked God to create in me a pure heart and renew my spirit.
Imma be humble when there's trouble I gotta stay clear of it.
The only sins that require two people are fornication & adultery.
I knew the Ten Commandments as a young adult now I'm free.
I gotta follow those laws so I won't walk in error with God.
If we worship God in spirit we gotta worship him in our heart.
We gotta worship God in our mind our hearts and our soul.
We gotta serve the Lord with our bodies he has to be in control.
I worship the Lord in spirit and in truth with total obedience everyday.
We worship God through Christ we show obedience when we pray.
Lord I feel so out of place when I don't feel you next to me.
Lord I feel hopelessly blind Lord I need your eyes to see.

Believe in Yourself

Philippians 4:4-Rejoice in the Lord always;
Again I say rejoice make a little time to give God praise.
Your attitude & confidence determines how well you succeed.
Knowing you accomplished your dreams makes my heart bleed.
You gotta acquire and obtain an instant winner's attitude.
Adopt a few positive habits that will change your mood.
Your mood comes first then your attitude is in second place.
Pick a phrase and use it every day a long side God's grace.
Believe in yourself look in the mirror and repeat that phrase.
Choose something simple that motivates you and give God praise.
I'm telling you it really is possible to feel really good everyday.
Repeat this phase Imma have a fantastic day everything will be ok.
Here's another one I can overcome any obstacle with God's grace.
Imma keep a positive attitude and Imma keep a smile on my face.
You'll get better as you go and you're getting wiser along the way.
You can reach your goals one step at a time every single day.
Everyday you're getting closer and closer to your goal.
If you believe it you can achieve it your future is about to unfold.
Everyday your mental attitude is becoming more positive.
You're starting to lose some weight and it will change how you live.
You're getting closer and closer to your goal of being trim and fit.
Believe in yourself you can be a winner if you just don't quit.
Rejoice in the Lord always and he'll give you courage and strength.
The devil can throw you a stumbling block and it won't make a dent.
My attitude makes me feel like I'm slim and about six feet tall.
But the truth is I'm not six feet and guess what I'm not slim at all.

Colossians: 1:3-We give thanks to God and the father our Lord.
That means Imma always pray for you to move forward.
You know God will always turn our mourning into joy.
So when Satan throws his darts you should know it's a decoy.
In Jesus name this too shall pass so send the devil on his way.
Whatever happens in life is caused by the words we say.
Satan I rebuke you in the Name of Jesus I refuse to worry.
I refuse to let anybody get my Father's praise or his glory.
Every sermon Jesus gave was powerful the devil is a joker.
The devil better back off and go somewhere and play poker.
We're gonna frustrate the devil and make him leave us alone.
He think he's gonna make me change my mind and do wrong.
Greater is he that is in me than he that is in the world.
He better think again I guess he didn't know I'm Wonder Girl.
The devil wonders what a girls gonna do next I'm not weak.
We overcome the devil by the blood and the words we speak.
There's nothing I'd like better than to frustrate the devil.
God has risen up a nation that will obey him on any level.
We can be bold enough to tell Satan to come on with it.
I'm in love with the Lord and a lot of people just don't get it.
When the children of God get together the devil will run.
I love the Lord I'm not afraid to tell the world what he's done.♥
I gotta testimony and Imma tell it from the mountain top.
You gotta believe in yourself and the blessing of God won't stop.
I get carried away about the Lord and people think I'm crazy.
I give the Lord unlimited praise because I'm energetic I'm not lazy.

Believe in Yourself

1 Thessalonians 5: 18 in everything give thanks its God's will.
I would like to tell you why I believe the Lord's love is real.
Many of us who want God's presence still remain weak.
It's immature to only want the Joy of the Lord and not be meek.
His presence will be the most precious gift we can receive.
There's still a battle that must be fought please don't deceive.
We need Warriors as well as Worshippers on the battle field.
That being said we can't be overcome by the devil's deal.
We gotta open our eyes because hell isn't a friendly fire.
We're on the same side seeking peace and our heart's desire.
Let us not slander one another but pray for understanding.
In order to stand together we gotta do some planning.
We gotta make time to meet for prayer often as we can.
Prayer will help us teach others and help them understand.
John the Baptist loved the Lord he had an apostolic voice.
His voice echoed in the hearts of people to repent and rejoice.
He instructed the people to make room for the Lord.
A voice of one calling in the wilderness seems to be a reward.
Prepare the way for the Lord make straight paths for him.
You may have many setbacks but don't let your soul go dim.
The Lord is our light and our salvation he gives us light.
Life including unsuccessful relationships but it's alright.
You may suffer emotional abuse a little fear and rejection.
That may cause low self-esteem and a bit of depression.
I was treated badly I wanted love that's all I thought of.
So I surrendered my life to Christ and embraced His love.

Pastor Deborah Wofford

2 Thessalonians 3:16 the Lord of peace himself give you peace always.
If you need some extra strength all you gotta do is give God praise.
I developed an intimate relationship with God which is cool.
I've learned that prayer is a weapon it's my best tool.
My vision for sisters of Destiny is to see them transformed.
You gotta present your body to Christ and not be conformed.
My vision for my brothers is for them to break the chain.
Let's birth our dreams and destinies so we can release pain.
We got goals to fulfill instead of out of wedlock babies.
Believe in yourself stop saying I can't stop all your maybes.
I want girls and boys all over the world to aim high and soar.
I really don't wanna see a bunch of dead dreams any more.
Fly like an eagle no matter what obstacles you may face.
Believe in yourself and be brave get up and join this race.
It don't matter where you been it matters where you're going.
Choose this day to move forward and start growing.
I'm Passionate about helping others reach their Destiny.
God called me to lose the shackles and set the captives free!
Your best days are before you no more looking back.
Press toward greatness and watch for God's mighty act.
I thank the Lord for the temporal blessings he handed me.
Like the refreshing air, the light of the sun, and my family.
The Lord gave me clothes and food that renews strength.
I appreciate my shelters and the love that keeps me content.
I appreciate the stars at night and the sleep that gives me rest.
I love the summer breeze and I love living without stress.

1-Timothy 6:7 for we brought nothing into this world; that's no doubt.
According to the word of God it is certain we can carry nothing out.
I appreciate the happy endearments of family and friends.
My cup runs over with joy since Jesus washed away my sins.
Suffer me not to be insensible to these daily mercies I relieve.
Lord your hand bestows blessings on me because I believe.
I escaped evil I bring my tribute of thanks for spiritual grace.
I got the full warmth of faith Jesus puts a smile on my face.
I enjoy the cheering presence of the Holy Spirit everyday.
The Lord gives me strength with a restraining will when I pray.
Let the redeemed of the Lord say so I have been redeemed.
The Lord done more for me then I could have ever dreamed.
From the hand of the enemy we get caught in the trials of life.
Then we forget what God did to get us through that old strife.
God sent his Son to us and bankrupted heaven to redeem us.
Satan had us in sin and God loves us so he gave us Jesus.
We have life so why don't we praise God and not complain.
If we praise God for all his works we'd drive the devil insane.
I love the Lord enough to pursue pure happiness with him.
If you really trust the Lord the chances of you failing is slim.
Dear Father I thank you for your love, kindness, and mercy.
Lord I really wanna thank you for your grace towards me.
Thank you for being such a faithful God and my deliverer.
Lord I really wanna thank you for being a faithful forgiver.
I exalt your Holy Name for the victory that I have in you.
Thank you for this glorious life and my window view.

Pastor Deborah Wofford

2-Timothy 1:7 for God hath not given us the spirit of fear.
Whatever you expect from the future will surely appear.
As I look through the mirror of your heart I see so much.
Lord I'm motivated and totally inspired by your sweet touch.
A conductor leads an orchestra with his back towards the crowd.
After each musical selection He faces them and He bowed.
That's pure confidence he doesn't wait for them to approve.
That's what you gotta do believe in yourself get up and move.
Remember when God orchestrated the heavens and the earth.
He admired His work and said this is good for all it's worth.
Believe in yourself you don't need anyone to validate you.
You're God's masterpiece so wake up and get yourself a clue.
He has created us new in Christ Jesus so what is the problem.
When God gives you a word, make sure you labor before Him.
Then his word can be birthed into your heart and you'll succeed.
Don't, move to the left or right before God give you what you need.
Wake up because you can do the right thing, in the wrong place.
And mess around and lose God's tender love, mercy and his grace.
Part of your maturation is your willingness to be patient always.
Don't get ahead of yourself, and by all means give God praise.
Remember don't move too fast you don't wanna get ahead of God.
You don't wanna move too fast and make things real hard.
Whatever God has spoken, He will surely bring it to pass.
Whatever our heavenly father decides to give us it will surely last.
Be still and know that God is God there's no limit to what he'll do.
Believe in yourself and be still and watch what God does for you.

Believe in Yourself

Titus 3:7 that being justified by his grace we should be made heirs.
According to the hope of eternal life we receive from our prayer.
When we pray we ask for forgiveness and receive salvation.
The Lord provides his unfailing love and grace without hesitation.
Listen my broadcast is coming in loud and very clear.
God's unconditional love will move you totally away from fear.
God's love will give you another level of understanding.
Don't touch that page! Now that's a little demanding.
We where made for his Glory and he want us to know him.
When you really love someone you will learn to trust them.
When you trust them you will learn to walk in that trust.
This is how we build a steady relationship with the Lord Jesus.
I travel life highway with the love and compassion God gave me.
I'm still amazed at all God done just to save and set me free.
God showed me his love and compassion like never before.
I understand it well no love no power no trust no get up and go.
When you have the love of Jesus Christ you can move on.
God's love will make all your fears disappear and be gone.
I wanna bring hope to those that are traveling this highway.
I'm singing the Lord praises and Imma stop right hear and pray.
The Jesus in me loves the Jesus in you together we are one.
We gotta tell the world what the Lord almighty God has done.
We have reached our potential goal with the fullness of God!
I won't be afraid to speak up even if it makes me feel odd.
I gotta job to do and I know exactly what needs to be done.
My father in heaven we continually give me strength to run.

Philemon 1:7 we have great joy and consolation in thy love.
Every good and perfect gift comes from the Lord up above.
Believe in yourself fear not my child for you are not alone
The Lord said he given you the most beautiful song.
I've walked beside you my child no doubt I've carried you.
Many nights I've quietly held you the whole night through.
Be not consumed with emptiness for I've filled you with light
Jesus said it's you he has chosen to shine ever so bright.
You struggled through the darkness without love & affection.
The Lord wants you to know him there's no more rejection.
This is where the Lord's abounds and takes your breath away.
No matter how things get the Lord will give you a better day.
You are a child of God lift up your head and walk ever boldly.
The Lord says he is our heavenly father and he made us holy.
Jesus is waiting for you reach out and grab the Lord's hand.
You wouldn't be able to smile without God or be able to stand.
With so many imaginations in life I never imagined Jesus love.
I never imagined what Jesus felt before going to heaven above.
I imagine going to heaven and seeing Jesus introduced to me.
I was amazed at what I don't see and amazed by what I do see.
The Lord allows us to see everything differently for a reason.
The same way he allows us to receive blessings in our own season.
We need to read the word of God and ask him for understanding.
When you know God's word in times of trouble you'll be left standing.
You gotta know what scriptures to use when it's time to put up a fight.
The Lord will not let you go to battle in darkness he'll give you light.

Believe in Yourself

Hebrew 11:6 but without faith it is impossible to please him.
If you don't trust and believe in the Lord there's a problem.
This world isn't our home our home is beyond the skies.
This world is filled will hate I got a love that never dies.
We are God's greatest creation we have power in our mind.
We have power over our thoughts I think about being kind.
God's love teaches me how to make people laugh and smile.
Believe in yourself be yourself others will admire your style.
Your Self Esteem and your Self Worth, is based on a feeling.
Laughter is a wonderful and delightful form of healing.
The Lord shed his blood for people all across the universe.
It's time for you to believe in yourself and put the Lord first.
The Lord called me righteous I'm under his control directly.
Jesus carries me in his arms so he can love and protect me.
You'll never know Jesus until you seek him and learn his will.
It's time to rediscover your life and realize Jesus is real.
God will give you knowledge and truth so you can surrender.
Once you're born again Jesus becomes your biggest defender.
Believe in yourself because the Lord already approved you.
Once you receive conformation from God you'll know it's true.
I seek God I preach so I can demonstrate what I believe.
I demonstrate what is pleasing to God in all I do and achieve.
Imma do what's acceptable to the Lord because I'm his child.
Imma be exceedingly pleasing to the Lord to make him smile.
Prayer lifts me up beyond hope when my methods fail.
The Lord gave me power to send the devil back to hell.

James 4:7 submit yourselves therefore to God resist the devil,
And he will flee from you; now let's head to the next level.
The devil will attack you at the worst time he hit's where it hurt.
The devil will attack you when you're in too much pain to be alert.
Someone is at the point of hopelessness the end of their rope.
A loved one is facing death the doctor said there's no hope.
Death seems inevitable especially when all hope is gone.
The miracle you prayed for isn't happening you feel alone.
Now the devil is attacking your mind with anger and fear.
You got overwhelming questions waiting for hope to appear.
Where is God now? You prayed there's no tears left to cry.
You fast for the promises of God your faith is about to die.
Blasphemy thoughts seem to bombard and invade your mind.
You're probably feeling like you done finally crossed the line.
Prayer failed your faith is gone you don't trust God anymore.
Don't question God because you don't know what to pray for.
These devices have been used by the devil for centuries.
When you resist the devil the Lord will set your mind at ease.
A lot of godly folks have been attacked by demonic forces.
The devil will flee when he hears a heart that rejoices.
If you go through the valley and the shadow of death don't fear.
Start praising God the devil will leave once he realizes hope is near.
Weeping will last for a few awful nights but joy is on the way.
In that darkness you'll hear the Lord whisper it's gonna be ok.
I can't explain faith or how it works one day it will make sense.
All I can say is the Lord will always leave you in suspense.

1 Peter 5:6 Humble-yourselves under the mighty hand of God.
God will exalt you in due time keep praying and stay on guard.
Humble yourself; and watch God's plan, put joy in your heart.
Whatever happened wasn't an accident or failure on your part.
Humble yourself under God's mighty hand pray and hold fast.
Let the Lord embrace you in all your pain his love will last.
The Lord has never failed his goodness and love carries me.
Believe in yourself let the Lord help you reach your destiny.
When all your human strength is gone God's love will prevail.
Be honest with yourself you know that you're doing quit well.
Hold fast to your faith let nothing cause you to live in doubt.
When it's all said and done you know God will work things out.
Stand on God's word don't let the devil make your head swirl.
Trust God especially when there's no other hope in this world.
I love the Lord I'm so glad he makes my heart and soul shine.
My soul may tremble but through it all I know Jesus is mine.
I was a wretched sinner until Jesus came along and set me free.
Through my pain Jesus held me and my soul still clings to Thee.
Believe in yourself pretty soon your faith will become strong.
Start trusting God more he'll put you right where you belong.
I dare you to step out on faith believe in yourself you are great.
Get up right now follow your heart don't wait until it's too late.
I know I owe the Lord everything I am and everything I'm not.
I know the Lord gave me life and he gave me everything I got.
The Lord gave me hope then he gave me a dream so I can live.
The Lord owns the world and he has so much more to give.

Pastor Deborah Wofford

2 Peter 1:2 Grace and peace be multiplied unto you,
Through the knowledge of God may he provide virtue?
Imagine knowing the Lord's will and having extra grace.
Imagine yourself being able to put a smile on the Lord's face.
With grace and peace multiplied you won't need to grieve.
There are so many things that grace and peace can relieve.
Your future is filled with love so no more feeling dismay.
You can rest the devil and all his workers are now cast away.
Our loving Father will never forsake those he love and created.
Dear friends our love for Jesus Christ is why we are so hated.
Don't let the work of your hands fade away with hopeless agony.
I won't let the devil's lies and destruction add more stress on me.
Dear friends pay attention listen the Lord's love is in your heart.
Bow to his wishes and do his will he won't let you fall apart.
There are millions of people that have surrendered to Jesus.
So they think but they haven't been converted or learned to trust.
They don't know the Lord the way the Lord should be known.
The greatest battle in the Church is everybody, wanna be on their own.
Jesus didn't come to bring religion he came to bring healing.
He came to bring salvation to those that are ready and willing.
Jesus came to re-establish what Adam lost Jesus came to restore.
He came to bring us back to fellowship so we can love God more.
Non-believers gotta work more jobs just to get what they need.
In the corporate world it is dog eat dog for people to succeed.
People usually step over each other in order to achieve success.
Everyone wants material gain but it all leads to a bunch of stress.

Believe in Yourself

1 John 1:9 if we confess our sins he is faithful and just to forgive.
A closer walk with the Lord will completely change how you live.
It's time for us to be more like our heavenly father in all our ways.
We're not like the world because God gave us a heart of praise.
We have to confess all our sins to the Lord when we do wrong.
Jesus won't leave us or forsake us he won't leave us alone.
I wanna comfort people everywhere in the USA and overseas.
I wanna set the captive free I wanna set your mind at ease.
Jesus made us his priority he can handle each and every problem.
The Lord gave some of us a special purpose to follow Him.
Jesus said seek first the kingdom of God and his righteousness.
We can't entertain the devil we gotta learn to fight without stress.
We the body of Christ gotta obey the commandments of the Lord.
You gotta believe in yourself and learn how to move forward.
You gotta obtain the knowledge of God and the truth and his will.
I'll preach inspiring messages reminding everyone Jesus can heal.
People try to display their level of bible knowledge on Sunday.
Then that wisdom and knowledge seem to quickly pass away.
We need to be reminded often what all we have waiting for us.
As long as we follow the commandments and obeyed Jesus.
Seeking the kingdom of God means seek heaven and God's will.
We gotta set our affection on things above God's love is real.
Christ sits at the right hand of God where we will be someday.
Believe in yourself and everything will turn out the right way.
I have a responsibility to give you hope and encourage you.
We're on earth with the responsibility of loving others with virtue.

2 John 1:7 for many deceivers has entered into the world, it's a mess.
They confess not that Jesus Christ is come in the flesh.
Believe in yourself because the Lord already approved you.
You won't know until you seek the Lord with loyalty and virtue.
You gotta believe in Christ and finally become a Christian.
Not by tradition and never rediscovering Jesus as a true friend.
You gotta learn the wisdom and knowledge and learn what's true.
Believe in yourself because God is preparing your breakthrough.
Seeking the Lord helps me demonstrate the calling on my life.
I live to seek aim and pursue my dreams without misery and strife.
I seek a life of righteousness I wanna continue living right.
I wanna serve the Lord with great joy consistently day and night.
God serves justice and mercy he gives everyone their just due.
I seek the Lord with compassion and I love serving others too.
I'm not the same as I was in the old days I put the past behind me.
I won't let my past hold me back any more I won't let it define me.
I'm so far from being perfect and a long ways from where I'm going.
When I get discouraged I realize I'm still learning and still growing.
There's no need for me to compete with the woman I use to be.
The only thing I need to remember is I can only control me.
I can't control your actions and you surely can't control mine.
Believe in yourself get motivated it's time to cross that line.
Life will bring you many heartaches ups and many more downs.
Just remember we all look much better without them serious frowns.
Don't let any one steal your joy and don't let anyone deceive you.
Believe in yourself it's time to show yourself exactly what you can do.

Believe in Yourself

3 John 1:4 I have no greater joy that to hear my children walk in truth.
We gotta share the word with everyone especially our youth.
Do you see hope when you look around at the world today.
You'll see there's a lack of sound judgment no one to pray.
Are we meeting the needs of the children we come in contact with?
Are we teaching them to love one another and never quit.
You gotta live according to God's way of doing and being right.
We gotta trust the Lord and know how to walk in his holy light.
Ultimately those who followed Jesus trusted him completely.
Some doubted what they didn't understand and didn't see,
Once you witness God's glory you can share Jesus Christ.
It's our job to share are wisdom and knowledge and give advice.
God looks past your theological background he'll set you free.
He doesn't look at your titles or your denominational pedigree.
Until you've repented you won't seer the Kingdom of God.
You must accept Jesus and be converted by giving him your heart.
The truth is without the Lord Jesus you will never be free.
You need the Lord to reveal those things that you can't see.
You shouldn't claim any form of Christian heritage nowadays.
All you need to do is concentrate on giving the Lord praise.
My friend the time as come for you to be converted lets repent.
The Kingdom of God is at hand the Father will give you strength.
God's plan is bigger than the theology that's passed down to us.
It goes from the blind leading the blind but we are lead by Jesus.
Our behavior has consequences so does the decisions we make.
God want his people to be different that's why he gives us breaks.

Jude 1: 25 to the only wise God our savior be-glory and majesty.
Imma serve the Lord with all my heart I can't have him mad at me.
Christ in you means the Holy Spirit lives inside of you.
You are the anointed one of God made whole made new.
You have tremendous potentials God gave you from birth.
God created man from dirt he created everything on earth.
Beneath the earth are tremendous resources like iron and brass.
Silver and gold may buy many things that surely won't last.
Jesus said those who believe in him will do greater works head.
With the power of Jesus you can heal the sick & raise the dead.
You can do things people call impossible through Jesus Christ.
Before God can use you to do these things you gotta sacrifice.
The Lord will break you don't just to make you whole again.
As you pass through his refining fire your new life will begin.
God will take you places that your mind will be in a complete daze.
Then all you can do is lift your hands and give God some praise.
God will take you from your normal state to a whole new level.
The Holy Spirit will help you to see straight through the devil.
When iron is extracted from the ground it's purified by fire.
Once the Lord purifies you he'll give you your hearts desire.
You gotta be refined so your gifts and talents can be in the limelight.
You'll have a testing of your faith just trust God you'll be alright.
If you haven't gone through trials believe me it's yet to come.
The Lord will show you where your help and support is from.
We all go through a fire or two I came out with glory on me.
With God's grace you can go through fiery tests victoriously.

Believe in Yourself

Revelation 7:16 they shall hunger no more neither thirst any more.
I love the Lord I can't wait to get to heaven that's all I live for.
Love yourself desire a change walk away from misery and strife.
Why read the word of the Lord and not apply it to your life.
My friend it's time to live and enjoy life Kick out the old ways.
Start practicing what you preach set your old life a blaze.
It's time for something new you gotta bring order to the chaos.
Get in order make time for prayer we gotta tie the devil up in knots.
Let the truth be your example let the Lord feed your soul.
Let your personal relationship with the Lord continue to unfold.
God will reveal the seasons in your life as you continue to sow.
Does the Lord make you feel like the sky is the limit as you grow?
Does he treat you like the most important person in the room?
Does he make you laugh when you feel empty and a little gloom?
Does he bring out the best in you does the Lord make you smile?
Does he make you believe in yourself because you're his child?
Does he motivate you to keep going when you don't understand?
Who do you really believe the word of God or the word of man?
When God speaks he gets things done and he has the last word.
He can make something out of nothing haven't you heard.
The birds and every beast enjoy the beauty of the skyline.
Believe in yourself with hope remember real faith is blind.
God specializes in making something out of nothing at all.
The Lord arms are long enough to catch you before you fall.
Believe in yourself pursue you dreams with all your heart.
The Lord will make your dreams come true if you do your part.

About The Author

Pastor Deborah Wofford is trying to build the body of Christ.
She's spreading hope and cheer with a whole lot of godly advice.
She encourage others with the struggles and pain she over came.
The one thing that's for sure is the power behind the Lord's holy name.
She said it's something about the Lord you really can't afford to miss.
Every time she in the presence of the Lord she feels pure joy and bliss.
She wants you to feel that great joy by getting on the Lord's team.
It's time for the children of the future to take back that dream.
God don't give up on her for what she did in the past long ago.
The Lord forgave her then the Lord gave her something to live for.
She finally realized that one accomplished dream leads to plenty.
If she can help at least one person she can and will help many.
The Lord told her to leave the past behind and look straight ahead.
That tape continued to play loud over and over in her head.
She started believing the Lord he was doing great things through her.
Motivated by the Lord she continually takes steps forward.
She made an oath to serve the Lord and happily do his will.
Sharing the message Jesus came to earth to restore and heal.
Determination and her passion for Jesus brought her a long way.
She made it through life with the desire to love God and pray.
Pastor Deborah Wofford mission is to inspire you and give you hope.
She knows exactly how it feels to be at the wrong end of the rope.